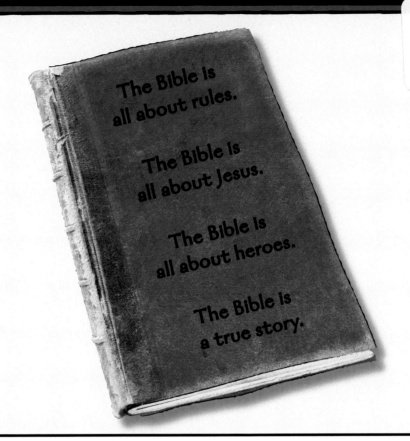

The Bible is all about rules.

The Bible is all about Jesus.

The Bible is all about heroes.

The Bible is a true story.

☺ Jesus in the Story

What did you discover about Jesus from this story? ⟶ **Jesus**

☺ A Verse from the Story to Learn at Home

In the beginning God created the heavens and the earth. (Genesis 1:1)

Genesis   Exodus   Leviticus   Numbers   Deuteronomy

Notes for parents: From the story we learned that the Bible is not mainly about us; it's about Jesus. It is not mainly about what we must do, but about what God has done.

Please help your child to memorize the verse and the Scripture reference for next time. Please review with them the place of the book of Genesis, using the diagram above.   www.jesusstorybookbible.com

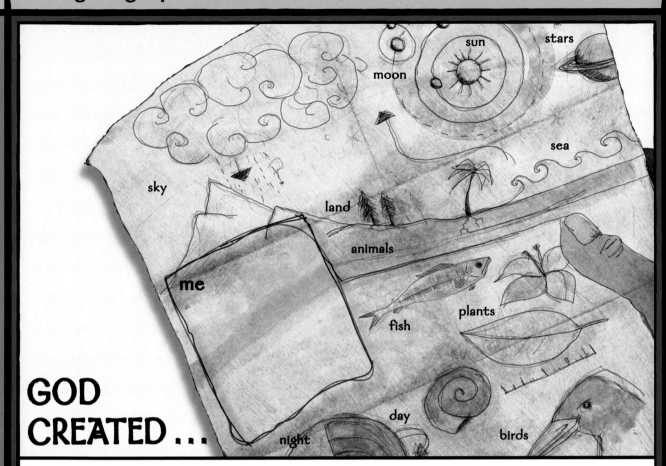

sun

moon

stars

sky

sea

land

animals

me

fish

plants

GOD
CREATED . . .

night

day

birds

☉ Jesus in the Story

What did you discover about
Jesus from this story?

⟶ Jesus

☉ A Verse from the Story to Learn at Home

In the beginning God created the heavens and the earth. (Genesis 1:1)

Genesis   Exodus   Leviticus   Numbers   Deuteronomy

Notes for parents: In today's story we learned that in the beginning God created everything and it was good.
Please help your child to memorize the verse and the Scripture reference for next time. Please review with them the
place of the book of Genesis, using the diagram above.   www.jesusstorybookbible.com

How much do you think God loved his people at the beginning, when the world was perfect?

1 2 3 4 5 6 7 8 9 10

How much do you think God loves his people now, when the world is NOT perfect?

1 2 3 4 5 6 7 8 9 10

☉ Jesus in the Story

What did you discover about Jesus from this story? ➔ Jesus

....

☉ A Verse from the Story to Learn at Home

The LORD saw that the human heart was only evil.
(Genesis 6:5)

Genesis   Exodus   Leviticus   Numbers   Deuteronomy

Notes for parents: From the story we learned that even though we don't always love God, he always loves us. God has a plan to solve the problem of sin, and the plan is Jesus.

Please help your child to memorize the verse and the Scripture reference for next time. Please review with them the place of the book of Genesis, using the diagram above.   www.jesusstorybookbible.com

How were Noah and his family rescued?

a) By being super swimmers.

b) By God.

Why were Noah and his family rescued?

a) Because they were good people.

b) Because God chose them.

What does God promise Noah?

a) That God would never again send a flood to destroy the world.

b) That God would give Noah fewer animals next time.

☉ Jesus in the Story

What did you discover about Jesus from this story? ⟶ Jesus

....

☉ A Verse from the Story to Learn at Home

The LORD saw that the human heart was only evil. (Genesis 6:5)

Genesis   Exodus   Leviticus   Numbers   Deuteronomy

Notes for parents: From the story we learned that God rescued Noah and his family because of his grace, not their goodness. We too are rescued because of God's grace.

Please help your child to memorize the verse and the Scripture reference for next time. Please review with them the place of the book of Genesis, using the diagram above.   www.jesusstorybookbible.com

Jesus in the Story

What did you discover about Jesus from this story?

Jesus

A Verse from the Story to Learn at Home

The LORD saw that the human heart was only evil.
(Genesis 6:5)

Genesis   Exodus   Leviticus   Numbers   Deuteronomy

Notes for parents: The people in the story thought they didn't need God and tried to get to heaven on their own. We learned that the way to heaven is not through something we do, but through a person — Jesus.
Please help your child to memorize the verse and the Scripture reference for next time. Please review with them the place of the book of Genesis, using the diagram above.
www.jesusstorybookbible.com

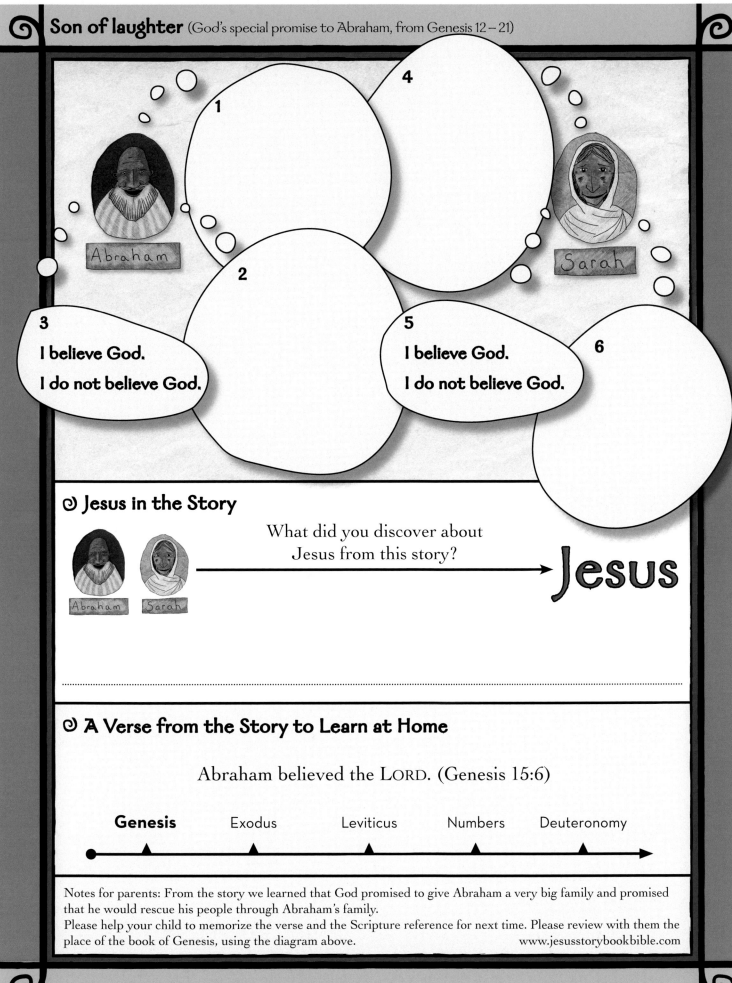

Jesus in the Story

What did you discover about Jesus from this story?

Abraham Sarah ────────────────▶ Jesus

A Verse from the Story to Learn at Home

Abraham believed the LORD. (Genesis 15:6)

Genesis   Exodus   Leviticus   Numbers   Deuteronomy

Notes for parents: From the story we learned that God promised to give Abraham a very big family and promised that he would rescue his people through Abraham's family.
Please help your child to memorize the verse and the Scripture reference for next time. Please review with them the place of the book of Genesis, using the diagram above.   www.jesusstorybookbible.com

Abraham was willing to give God his only son whom he loved, why?

Abraham trusted God and l __ __ __ __ God more than anything else.

What did God provide for the sacrifice instead of Isaac?

A r __ __ .

What did Abraham do with the ram?

Abraham sacrificed the ram

instead of his s __ __ .

☉ Jesus in the Story

What did you discover about
Jesus from this story?

———————➤ Jesus

....

☉ A Verse from the Story to Learn at Home

Abraham believed the LORD. (Genesis 15:6)

Genesis   Exodus   Leviticus   Numbers   Deuteronomy

●——▲————▲————▲————▲————▲——————➤

Notes for parents: From the story we learned that Abraham was asked to give up something he really loved — his only son, Isaac. God provided a sacrifice in Isaac's place. God later provided the ultimate sacrifice, his only Son, Jesus. Please help your child to memorize the verse and the Scripture reference for next time. Please review with them the place of the book of Genesis, using the diagram above.   www.jesusstorybookbible.com

Jesus in the Story

What did you discover about Jesus from this story? ⟶ Jesus

A Verse from the Story to Learn at Home

You intended to harm me, but God intended it for good.
(Genesis 50:20)

Genesis   Exodus   Leviticus   Numbers   Deuteronomy

Notes for parents: From the story we learned about how God often sets his love on and does amazing things through people who are unloved, unwanted, unattractive, and unpopular — just like Leah and just like Jesus. Please help your child to memorize the verse and the Scripture reference for next time. Please review with them the place of the book of Genesis, using the diagram above.   www.jesusstorybookbible.com

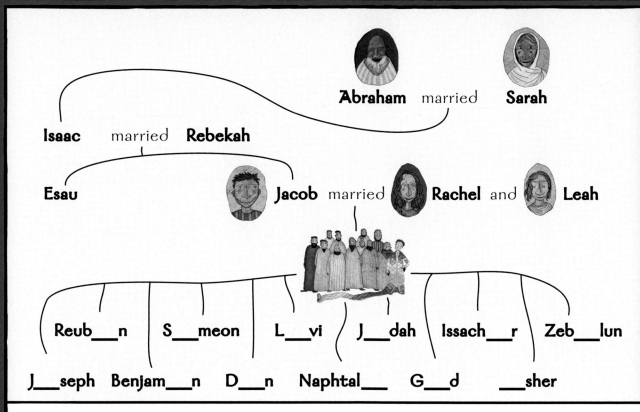

Abraham married Sarah

Isaac married Rebekah

Esau Jacob married Rachel and Leah

Reub__n · S__meon · L__vi · J__dah · Issach__r · Zeb__lun

J__seph Benjam__n D__n Naphtal__ G__d __sher

☺ Jesus in the Story

What did you discover about Jesus from this story?

Jesus

....

☺ A Verse from the Story to Learn at Home

You intended to harm me, but God intended it for good.
(Genesis 50:20)

Genesis   Exodus   Leviticus   Numbers   Deuteronomy

Notes for parents: From the story we learned that Joseph was betrayed and rejected by his brothers but, by God's plan, Joseph later rescued them. Jesus was betrayed and rejected but, by God's plan, rescued us. God is always in control. Please help your child to memorize the verse and the Scripture reference for next time. Please review with them the place of the book of Genesis, using the diagram above.   www.jesusstorybookbible.com

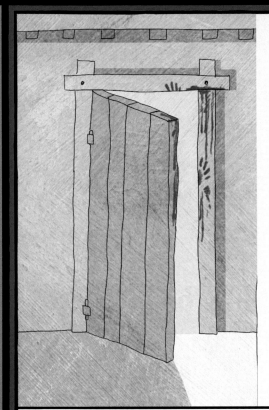

QXTZHQEXLQQAZMXXBDZ
QIXEZXDZZIXXNQXSXTZE
XAXDOQXFZMXEQZ

___ ____ ____

_____

__ __ !

☽ Jesus in the Story

What did you discover about
Jesus from this story? ⟶ Jesus

....

☽ A Verse from the Story to Learn at Home

God said, "I will take you as my own people, and I will be your God."
(Exodus 6:7)

| Genesis | **Exodus** | Leviticus | Numbers | Deuteronomy |

Notes for parents: From the story we learned about the first Passover, where a lamb was sacrificed to rescue God's people. Jesus is called the Lamb of God, because he was sacrificed to rescue us.
Please help your child to memorize the verse and the Scripture reference for next time. Please review with them the place of the book of Exodus, using the diagram above.   www.jesusstorybookbible.com

God is . . .

_____!

☊ Jesus in the Story

What did you discover about
Jesus from this story?

→ **Jesus**

....

☊ A Verse from the Story to Learn at Home

God said, "I will take you as my own people, and I will be your God."
(Exodus 6:7)

| Genesis | **Exodus** | Leviticus | Numbers | Deuteronomy |

Notes for parents: From the story we learned about how God rescued his people by making a way through the Red Sea. One day there would be an even greater rescue — Jesus dying on the cross.
Please help your child to memorize the verse and the Scripture reference for next time. Please review with them the place of the book of Exodus, using the diagram above.
www.jesusstorybookbible.com

Ten ways to be perfect (Moses and the Ten Commandments, from Exodus 16 – 17, 19 – 40)

Do you have something that you sometimes treat as more important to you than God?

_____

You shall have no other gods before me.

You shall not make for yourself an idol.

You shall not misuse the name of the LORD your God.

Remember the Sabbath day by keeping it holy.

Honor your father and your mother.

You shall not murder.

You shall not commit adultery.

You shall not steal.

You shall not lie.

You shall not covet.

The people promised always to obey the Ten Commandments. Can they keep their promise?

YES   NO

Does obeying the Ten Commandments save people?

YES   NO

Does God save people?

YES   NO

☉ Jesus in the Story

What did you discover about Jesus from this story?

→ Jesus

....

☉ A Verse from the Story to Learn at Home

You shall have no other gods before me. (Exodus 20:3)

Genesis   **Exodus**   Leviticus   Numbers   Deuteronomy

Notes for parents: From the story we learned that God gave his people the Ten Commandments. But the people couldn't keep the commandments. Only one person obeyed all of God's commandments all the time — Jesus. Please help your child to memorize the verse and the Scripture reference for next time. Please review with them the place of the book of Exodus, using the diagram above.   www.jesusstorybookbible.com

What does God promise his people?

a) That he will never be with them.

b) That he will always be with them.

c) That he will sometimes be with them.

Why were Joshua and the people able to enter Jericho?

a) Because they had a great big army.

b) Because they were good at marching.

c) Because God was with them.

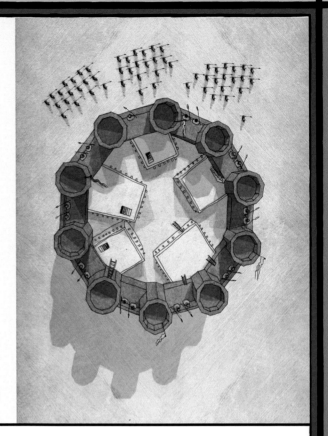

☉ Jesus in the Story

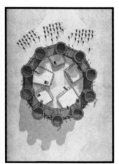

What did you discover about
Jesus from this story?

➔ Jesus

☉ A Verse from the Story to Learn at Home

You shall have no other gods before me. (Exodus 20:3)

| Genesis | **Exodus** | Leviticus | Numbers | Deuteronomy |

Notes for parents: From the story we learned that Joshua and the people obeyed God. God made the walls of Jericho fall down and led them into their new home. God promised to always be with them. God will always be with us too, and we too must obey God.

Please help your child to memorize the verse and the Scripture reference for next time. Please review with them the place of the book of Exodus, using the diagram above.   www.jesusstorybookbible.com

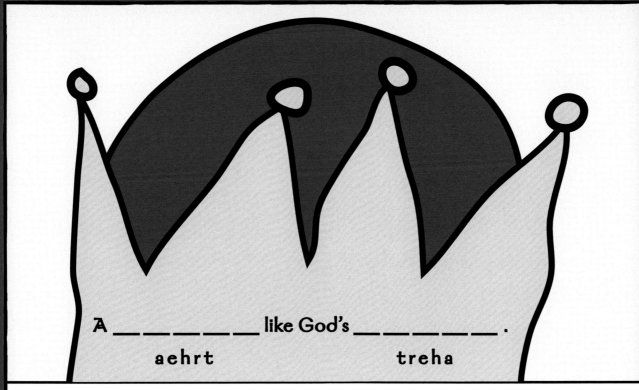

A _ _ _ _ _ _ _ like God's _ _ _ _ _ _ .
    aehrt   treha

☾ Jesus in the Story

What did you discover about
Jesus from this story? ⟶ Jesus

....

☾ A Verse from the Story to Learn at Home

I keep my eyes always on the LORD. I will not be shaken.
(Psalm 16:8)

Esther   Job   **Psalms**   Proverbs   Ecclesiastes

⟵ ▲   ▲   ▲   ▲   ▲ ⟶

Notes for parents: From the story we learned that God chose David to be king. God was getting his people ready for an even greater King — Jesus.

Please help your child to memorize the verse and the Scripture reference for next time. Please review with them the place of the book of Psalms, using the diagram above. For next time, if possible, please also give your child a cardboard box (e.g., a shoebox or tissue box) for the craft.   www.jesusstorybookbible.com

Did David believe he could beat Goliath by himself?   YES   NO

Did David think being strong saves you?   YES   NO

Did his own strength give David true courage?   YES   NO

Did God give David true courage?   YES   NO

Is it strength that will save you?   YES   NO

Is it God that will save you?   YES   NO

☉ Jesus in the Story

What did you discover about
Jesus from this story?   ⟶   Jesus

....

☉ A Verse from the Story to Learn at Home

I keep my eyes always on the LORD. I will not be shaken.
(Psalm 16:8)

Esther   Job   **Psalms**   Proverbs   Ecclesiastes

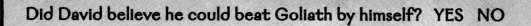

Notes for parents: From the story we learned that David had true courage because he knew that it is God that saves. We also learned that God sent David to save the people from Goliath and God sends Jesus to save us. Please help your child to memorize the verse and the Scripture reference for next time. Please review with them the place of the book of Psalms, using the diagram above.   www.jesusstorybookbible.com

The LORD is my ___ __ __ __ __ __ __ __ .

I lack nothing. He makes me lie down in green pastures, he leads me beside quiet waters, he refreshes my soul.

He guides me along the right paths for his name's sake.

Even though I walk through the darkest valley, I will fear no evil, for you are with me; your rod and your staff, they comfort me.

You prepare a table before me in the presence of my enemies.

You anoint my head with oil; my cup overflows.

Surely your goodness and love will follow me all the days of my life, and I will dwell in the house of the LORD forever.

☉ Jesus in the Story

What did you discover about
Jesus from this story?

Jesus

....

☉ A Verse from the Story to Learn at Home

I keep my eyes always on the LORD. I will not be shaken.
(Psalm 16:8)

| Esther | Job | **Psalms** | Proverbs | Ecclesiastes |

Notes for parents: From Psalm 23 we learned that we, like sheep, need someone to take care of us and rescue us. Jesus is the Good Shepherd.

Please help your child to memorize the verse and the Scripture reference for next time. Please review with them the place of the book of Psalms, using the diagram above. www.jesusstorybookbible.com

How did Naaman think he would be saved?

a) By going to see the king.

b) By doing something important.

c) By a free gift from God.

How was Naaman saved?

a) By going to see the king.

b) By doing something important.

c) By a free gift from God.

How are people today saved?

a) By going to church, reading their Bible, and praying.

b) By doing something important.

c) By a free gift from God.

◎ Jesus in the Story

What did you discover about
Jesus from this story? ⟶ Jesus

....

◎ A Verse from the Story to Learn at Home

The LORD has laid on him the sin of us all. (Isaiah 53:6)

Ecclesiastes   Song of Songs   **Isaiah**   Jeremiah   Lamentations

⟵————▲————————▲————————▲————————▲————————▲————⟶

Notes for parents: From the story we learned that Naaman thought God would save him because of how important he was. But God saves us because of what Jesus has done. It is a free gift.

Please help your child to memorize the verse and the Scripture reference for next time. Please review with them the place of the book of Isaiah, using the diagram above.   www.jesusstorybookbible.com

Wonderful Counselor

King

Royal Son

Servant

Shepherd

Mighty God

Rescuer

Everlasting Father

Lamb

Hero

Prince of Peace

Emmanuel

Light

☉ Jesus in the Story

What did you discover about
Jesus from this story?

→ Jesus

....

☉ A Verse from the Story to Learn at Home

The LORD has laid on him the sin of us all. (Isaiah 53:6)

Ecclesiastes   Song of Songs   **Isaiah**   Jeremiah   Lamentations

◄———▲————————▲————————▲————————▲————————▲———————►

Notes for parents: From the story we learned that God told Isaiah about a future Rescuer King who will come to earth and do many amazing things, but then he will suffer and die. But God will make him alive again, and he will rescue his people and one day make the world perfect again.

Please help your child to memorize the verse and the Scripture reference for next time. Please review with them the place of the book of Isaiah, using the diagram above.   www.jesusstorybookbible.com

☙ Jesus in the Story

 What did you discover about Jesus from this story? ⟶ Jesus

....

☙ A Verse from the Story to Learn at Home

Salvation comes from the LORD. (Jonah 2:9)

Amos — Obadiah — **Jonah** — Micah — Nahum

←————▲————————▲————————▲————————▲————————▲————→

Notes for parents: From the story we learned that Daniel obeyed God even though he knew it would cost him. We also learned that Jesus would obey God, whatever it cost, even if it meant he would die.
Please help your child to memorize the verse and the Scripture reference for next time. Please review with them the place of the book of Jonah, using the diagram above.   www.jesusstorybookbible.com

God said:

"The people have run away from me,

but I still _____ them."

Jonah said:

"Those are bad people doing bad things,

I do not _____ them."

☉ Jesus in the Story

What did you discover about
Jesus from this story?

→ Jesus

....

☉ A Verse from the Story to Learn at Home

Salvation comes from the LORD. (Jonah 2:9)

Amos	Obadiah	**Jonah**	Micah	Nahum

←——————————————————————————→

Notes for parents: From the story we learned that God loved the people of Nineveh. Even though we sin and run away from God, he still loves us and wants to forgive us.
Please help your child to memorize the verse and the Scripture reference for next time. Please review with them the place of the book of Jonah, using the diagram above.   www.jesusstorybookbible.com

God's people were . . .

a) . . . able to keep God's rules.

b) . . . not able to keep God's rules.

God's people are saved by . . .

a) . . . keeping God's rules.

b) . . . a Rescuer.

☺ Jesus in the Story

What did you discover about
Jesus from this story?

Jesus

....

☺ To Learn at Home

Matthew	→	1 Corinthians	→	1 Thessalonians	→	Hebrews	→	3 John
Mark		2 Corinthians		2 Thessalonians		James		Jude
Luke		Galatians		1 Timothy		1 Peter		Revelation
John		Ephesians		2 Timothy		2 Peter		
Acts		Philippians		Titus		1 John		
Romans		Colossians		Philemon		2 John		

Notes for parents: As we finished the Old Testament, we remembered how it points to God's great plan to rescue his people. God will provide a Rescuer — Jesus.

Please help your child to memorize the names and order of the books of the New Testament.

www.jesusstorybookbible.com